The Fearless Netpreneur's

FUNNEL CREATION MANIFESTO

Step By Step Breakdown Of Different Marketing Funnel Strategies, Tools & Resources You Need To Create And Deploy Them For Maximum Profits

Dr. Ope Banwo

Copyright Page

First Edition: 2024

Printed in Omaha Nebraska USA

Publisher: Netpreneur360.com

Library of Congress Cataloging-in-Publication Data:

Funnel Creation Manifesto / Dr. Ope Banwo

The information presented in this book reflects the author's views at the time of publication. This book is provided as step-by-step breakdown of different marketing funnel strategy you need to deploy to make profit in digital business.

Contents

About the Author

Dr. Ope Banwo is a renowned digital business strategist, entrepreneur, and motivational speaker with a passion for empowering individuals and businesses to achieve their full potential. Based in Omaha, Nebraska, USA, Dr. Banwo has carved out a distinguished career as an expert in marketing funnels, online business development, and digital transformation.

With over two decades of experience, Dr. Banwo has successfully founded and managed several digital companies, providing innovative solutions to entrepreneurs and businesses worldwide. He is the visionary behind multiple online marketing courses, webinars, and workshops that have helped thousands of people navigate the complexities of the digital marketplace.

Dr. Banwo holds advanced degrees in law and business administration, which he leverages to offer a unique blend of legal and entrepreneurial insights. His dynamic approach to digital marketing and business growth has earned him recognition as a thought leader in the industry.

A prolific author, Dr. Banwo has written numerous books and articles on digital marketing, personal development, and business strategies. His work is characterized by practical advice, inspirational guidance, and a commitment to ethical business practices.

Dedicated to sharing his knowledge, Dr. Banwo regularly speaks at international conferences and events, inspiring audiences with his innovative ideas and success stories. His mission is to empower others to create sustainable and profitable online businesses while maintaining their integrity and values.

For more information and resources from Dr. Ope Banwo, visit his official website and join his community of motivated entrepreneurs.

Why I Wrote This Manifesto

As a digital business strategist with over two decades of experience, I have witnessed firsthand the transformative power of an effective marketing funnel. The digital landscape is ever-evolving, and many entrepreneurs and businesses struggle to navigate its complexities. I wrote Funnel Creation Manifesto to provide a clear, actionable guide that demystifies the marketing funnel process and empowers you to harness its potential for your business.

I have always been passionate about helping others achieve their full potential in the digital marketplace. Throughout my career, I have seen countless businesses fail not because they lacked a great product or service, but because they did not have a well-structured marketing strategy. This manifesto is my way of sharing the knowledge and insights I have gained, helping you avoid common pitfalls and succeed where others have stumbled.

The concept of a marketing funnel is not new, but its application in the digital age requires a fresh perspective and innovative approaches. In this manifesto, I break down the key stages of a marketing funnel—Awareness, Interest, Decision, Action, and Retention—and provide practical tips and strategies for each phase. My goal is to equip you with the tools and understanding necessary to attract, engage, and retain customers effectively.

Moreover, I believe in the importance of ethical business practices and maintaining integrity in all endeavors. This manifesto not only focuses on achieving financial success but also emphasizes the importance of building lasting relationships with your customers and creating value in their lives.

Funnel Creation Manifesto is a culmination of my experiences, successes, and lessons learned. It is a comprehensive guide designed to help you build a sustainable and profitable online business. Whether you are a seasoned entrepreneur or just starting out, this manifesto will provide you with the insights and strategies needed to thrive in the digital world.

Thank you for joining me on this journey. I am excited to see how you will apply these principles to your business and achieve remarkable success.

MODULE 1: What is a Marketing Funnel in Digital Business?

A marketing funnel, also known as a sales funnel or conversion funnel, is a strategic model that represents the journey a potential customer takes from the first interaction with your business to the final purchase and beyond. It visually outlines each step a prospect goes through, guiding them from awareness to interest, decision, and action. The funnel metaphor is used because, like a funnel, it starts wide at the top, capturing a broad audience, and narrows down as potential customers move closer to making a purchase.

Key Stages of a Marketing Funnel:

1. **Awareness:** The top of the funnel (TOFU) where potential customers become aware of your brand through various channels like social media, blogs, SEO, and ads.

2. **Interest:** The middle of the funnel (MOFU) where prospects show interest in your products or services and seek more information. This stage often involves content marketing, email newsletters, and webinars.

3. **Decision:** The bottom of the funnel (BOFU) where prospects are considering making a purchase. Here, businesses provide detailed information, testimonials, case studies, and special offers to help prospects make a decision.

4. **Action:** The final stage where the prospect makes a purchase or converts. This stage may also include upselling and cross-selling strategies.

5. **Retention:** Post-purchase activities aimed at retaining customers and turning them into repeat buyers and brand advocates.

Major Benefits of Having a Highly Converting Funnel

1. Increased Conversion Rates:

A well-structured funnel guides potential customers through the buying process, addressing their concerns and providing relevant information at each stage, which significantly increases the likelihood of conversion.

2. Better Customer Insights:

Funnels allow you to track and analyze customer behavior at each stage, providing valuable insights into what works and what doesn't. This data can be used to optimize marketing strategies and improve customer targeting.

3. Improved Customer Experience:

By delivering personalized content and offers at the right time, funnels enhance the customer experience, making it more likely that prospects will trust your brand and make a purchase.

4. Effective Resource Allocation:

Funnels help you identify which marketing strategies and channels yield the best results, allowing you to allocate resources more effectively and maximize your return on investment (ROI).

5. Enhanced Brand Loyalty:

By nurturing leads and providing value at every stage, funnels help build stronger relationships with customers, leading to increased brand loyalty and repeat business.

6. Scalability:

Once established, a highly converting funnel can be scaled to handle larger volumes of traffic, allowing your business to grow without a proportional increase in marketing costs.

7. Automation Opportunities:

Many elements of a marketing funnel can be automated, such as email marketing campaigns and lead nurturing sequences. This saves time and ensures consistent communication with prospects.

8. Predictable Revenue:

A well-optimized funnel provides a predictable flow of leads and conversions, making it easier to forecast revenue and plan for business growth.

Why Every Digital Business Should Have a Marketing Funnel

1. Systematic Lead Generation:

A marketing funnel creates a systematic approach to generating and nurturing leads, ensuring that no potential customer falls through the cracks.

2. Maximized Marketing Efforts:

By guiding prospects through a defined journey, funnels maximize the impact of your marketing efforts, ensuring that each touchpoint moves them closer to a purchase.

3. Competitive Advantage:

Businesses with well-optimized funnels often outperform competitors by converting more prospects into customers and building stronger relationships with their audience.

4. Cost Efficiency:

Funnels help in identifying and focusing on high-value leads, reducing the cost of customer acquisition and increasing the efficiency of your marketing budget.

5. Long-Term Business Growth:

A highly converting funnel not only boosts immediate sales but also lays the foundation for long-term business growth through customer retention and loyalty.

By implementing and continuously optimizing a marketing funnel, digital businesses can create a seamless and effective pathway for turning prospects into loyal customers, driving sustained growth and success.

MODULE 2: Types of Marketing Funnels

There are several types of marketing funnels, each tailored to different business goals and customer journeys. Here's an overview of the main types of marketing funnels, what they do, and when they are appropriate to use:

1. Lead Generation Funnel

- *What It Does:* Captures leads by offering valuable content in exchange for contact information.

- *When to Use:* When you want to build your email list or database of potential customers for future marketing efforts.

- *Typical Components:* Landing page with a lead magnet (e.g., eBook, webinar, free trial), opt-in form, thank you page, and follow-up email sequence.

2. Sales Funnel

- *What It Does:* Guides potential customers through the buying process to make a purchase.

- *When to Use:* When you have a product or service to sell directly to consumers or businesses.

- *Typical Components:* Sales page, product information, testimonials, pricing details, checkout page, order confirmation page, and post-purchase follow-up emails.

3. Webinar Funnel

- *What It Does:* Attracts and engages potential customers through an educational or informative webinar, leading to a sales offer.

- *When to Use:* When you want to build authority, educate your audience, and sell high-ticket products or services.

- *Typical Components:* Registration page, confirmation page, reminder emails, live or recorded webinar, sales page with a special offer, and follow-up emails.

4. Product Launch Funnel

- *What It Does:* Builds anticipation and excitement for a new product launch, culminating in sales.

- *When to Use:* When launching a new product or service.

- *Typical Components:* Pre-launch content pages, landing page for early access sign-ups, sales page, launch emails, and upsell/cross-sell pages.

5. Tripwire Funnel

- *What It Does:* Converts leads into customers by offering a low-cost product (tripwire) to encourage an initial purchase, followed by upsells and cross-sells.

- *When to Use:* When you want to quickly turn leads into paying customers and increase the average customer value.

- *Typical Components:* Lead magnet landing page, tripwire sales page, upsell pages, and follow-up emails.

6. Squeeze Page Funnel

- *What It Does:* Captures email addresses through a highly focused landing page with minimal distractions.

- *When to Use:* When you want to grow your email list quickly.

- *Typical Components:* Squeeze page with a clear, concise offer, opt-in form, and thank you page.

7. Free Plus Shipping Funnel

- *What It Does:* Offers a free physical product with the customer only paying for shipping, leading to upsells and cross-sells.

- *When to Use:* When you want to acquire new customers with a low entry barrier and increase their lifetime value.

- *Typical Components:* Free plus shipping offer page, checkout page, upsell pages, and follow-up emails.

8. Consultation Funnel

- *What It Does:* Captures leads and encourages them to book a consultation or discovery call.

- *When to Use:* When selling high-ticket services or personalized solutions.

- *Typical Components:* Landing page with a call-to-action to book a consultation, application or booking form, thank you page, and follow-up emails.

9. Membership Funnel

- *What It Does:* Encourages leads to sign up for a membership site or subscription service.

- *When to Use:* When you offer ongoing value through a membership or subscription model.

- *Typical Components:* Membership sales page, pricing details, registration page, welcome email, and member onboarding sequence.

Summary of Marketing Funnel Types and Their Uses:

1. **Lead Generation Funnel:** Captures leads for future marketing; use when building your email list.

2. **Sales Funnel:** Converts visitors to buyers; use when selling products or services.

3. **Webinar Funnel:** Educates and sells through webinars; use for high-ticket items.

4. **Product Launch Funnel:** Builds anticipation and drives sales; use for new product launches.

5. Tripwire Funnel: Converts leads to customers with a low-cost offer; use to increase customer value quickly.

6. Squeeze Page Funnel: Captures email addresses rapidly; use to grow your email list.

7. Free Plus Shipping Funnel: Acquires customers with a low-cost entry; use to build customer base.

8. Consultation Funnel: Books consultations for high-ticket services; use for personalized solutions.

9. Membership Funnel: Grows membership or subscription base; use for ongoing value offerings.

Each type of funnel is designed to achieve specific business objectives and can be used strategically depending on your goals and the nature of your offerings.

I can provide a textual representation of the graphic here, and you might consider using a graphic design tool to create a visual based on this description.

Visual Representation of Marketing Funnels

1. Lead Generation Funnel:

   - *Landing Page* → *Opt-In Form* → *Thank You Page*

2. Sales Funnel:

   - *Sales Page* → *Product Information* → *Checkout Page* → *Order Confirmation Page*

3. Webinar Funnel:

   - *Registration Page* → *Confirmation Page* → *Webinar* → *Sales Page*

4. Product Launch Funnel:

   - *Pre-Launch Content Pages* → *Landing Page* → *Sales Page* → *Launch Emails*

5. Tripwire Funnel:

   - *Lead Magnet* → *Tripwire Sales Page* → *Upsell Pages*

6. Squeeze Page Funnel:

   - *Squeeze Page* → *Opt-In Form* → *Thank You Page*

7. Free Plus Shipping Funnel:

   - *Offer Page* → *Checkout Page* → *Upsell Pages*

8. Consultation Funnel:

   - *Landing Page* → *Booking Form* → *Thank You Page*

9. Membership Funnel:

   - *Membership Sales Page* → *Registration Page* → *Onboarding Sequence*

You can visualize each funnel as a flowchart where each arrow (→) represents the progression from one component to the next within the funnel. Here is a simple text flow to help you get started:

Lead Generation Funnel

Landing Page → Opt-In Form → Thank You Page

Sales Funnel

Sales Page → Product Information → Checkout Page → Order Confirmation Page

Webinar Funnel

Registration Page → Confirmation Page → Webinar → Sales Page

Product Launch Funnel

Pre-Launch Content Pages → Landing Page → Sales Page → Launch Emails

Tripwire Funnel

Lead Magnet → Tripwire Sales Page → Upsell Pages

Squeeze Page Funnel

Squeeze Page → Opt-In Form → Thank You Page

Free Plus Shipping Funnel

Offer Page → Checkout Page → Upsell Pages

Consultation Funnel

Landing Page → Booking Form → Thank You Page

Membership Funnel

Membership Sales Page → Registration Page → Onboarding Sequence

Using a graphic design tool, you can create boxes for each component and connect them with arrows to visually represent each funnel type.

MODULE 3: Main Stages of a Marketing Funnel Structure

A marketing funnel structure typically comprises several key stages that guide potential customers from initial awareness to final conversion and beyond. Here are the main stages:

1. Awareness

- *Goal:* To attract and capture the attention of a broad audience.

- *Tactics:* Content marketing, social media posts, SEO, paid ads, influencer marketing, webinars, and public relations.

- *Activities:* Blog posts, videos, infographics, social media content, and advertisements that introduce the brand and its offerings.

2. Interest

- *Goal:* To engage the audience and generate interest in your products or services.

- *Tactics:* Email marketing, lead magnets (e.g., eBooks, whitepapers), informative content, webinars, and free trials.

- *Activities:* Sending newsletters, offering downloadable resources, hosting webinars, and creating educational content that provides value and encourages prospects to learn more.

3. Consideration

- *Goal:* To nurture leads and build trust, helping prospects evaluate your offerings.

- *Tactics:* Detailed product information, case studies, testimonials, comparison guides, and free demos.

- *Activities:* Sharing customer success stories, providing product demos or trials, offering detailed product descriptions, and creating comparison charts.

4. Intent

- *Goal:* To move prospects closer to making a purchase decision.

- *Tactics:* Personalized email campaigns, remarketing ads, product recommendations, and limited-time offers.

- *Activities:* Sending personalized emails, showcasing user reviews and ratings, providing targeted product recommendations, and offering special discounts or promotions.

5. Evaluation

- *Goal:* To address any final objections and encourage conversion.

- *Tactics:* Sales calls, live chats, detailed FAQs, and customer support.

- *Activities:* Engaging in direct communication with potential customers, answering their questions, addressing concerns, and providing clear, compelling reasons to choose your product.

6. Purchase

- *Goal:* To facilitate the final purchase decision and conversion.

- *Tactics:* Streamlined checkout processes, secure payment options, and confirmation emails.

- *Activities:* Offering a simple and intuitive purchase process, providing various payment methods, sending order confirmation emails, and thanking customers for their purchase.

7. Post-Purchase (Retention)

- *Goal:* To retain customers and encourage repeat business and loyalty.

- *Tactics:* Follow-up emails, loyalty programs, personalized recommendations, and customer satisfaction surveys.

- *Activities:* Sending thank-you emails, offering loyalty rewards, providing personalized product recommendations, and seeking feedback through surveys.

8. Advocacy

- *Goal:* To turn satisfied customers into brand advocates who promote your business.

- *Tactics:* Referral programs, social proof campaigns, and user-generated content.

- *Activities:* Encouraging customers to leave reviews, sharing user-generated content on social media, offering referral incentives, and highlighting customer testimonials.

Summary of Marketing Funnel Stages:

1. **Awareness:** Attracting potential customers.

2. **Interest:** Engaging and generating interest.

3. **Consideration:** Nurturing leads and building trust.

4. **Intent:** Moving prospects closer to purchase.

5. **Evaluation:** Addressing objections and encouraging conversion.

6. **Purchase:** Facilitating the final purchase decision.

7. **Post-Purchase (Retention):** Retaining customers and encouraging repeat business.

8. **Advocacy:** Turning satisfied customers into brand advocates.

By understanding and effectively managing these stages, businesses can create a seamless customer journey that maximizes conversions and fosters long-term customer relationships.

MODULE 4: Webpages Needed for a Product Launch Funnel

A product launch funnel consists of several key webpages designed to guide potential customers through the journey from awareness to purchase. Here are the different webpages you need for a successful product launch funnel:

1. Pre-Launch Content Pages

- *Purpose:* To generate buzz and build anticipation for the upcoming product launch.

- *Content:* Teaser information, sneak peeks, and early insights about the product.

- *Features:* Sign-up forms to capture email addresses for early access or exclusive updates.

2. Landing Page

- *Purpose:* To capture leads and convert visitors into potential buyers.

- *Content:* Compelling headline, product benefits, high-quality images, and a clear call-to-action (CTA).

- *Features:* Lead capture form, testimonials, and a value proposition highlighting why visitors should be interested.

3. Thank You Page (for Lead Capture)

- *Purpose:* To acknowledge the lead capture and provide next steps.

- *Content:* Thank you message, what to expect next, and possibly a special offer or discount for early adopters.

- *Features:* Links to additional content or social media for further engagement.

4. Sales Page

- *Purpose:* To provide detailed information about the product and persuade visitors to make a purchase.

- *Content:* In-depth product description, features, benefits, high-quality images, videos, testimonials, and case studies.

- *Features:* Strong CTAs, pricing information, payment options, and a purchase button.

5. Checkout Page

- *Purpose:* To facilitate the final purchase process.

- *Content:* Order summary, billing and shipping details, and payment options.

- *Features:* Secure payment gateway, progress indicators, and trust signals (e.g., security badges).

6. Order Confirmation Page

- *Purpose:* To confirm the order and provide a summary of the purchase.

- *Content:* Thank you message, order details, expected delivery information, and customer service contact information.

- *Features:* Links to further product recommendations or user guides.

7. Upsell/Cross-Sell Page

- *Purpose:* To increase the average order value by offering additional products or upgrades.

- *Content:* Additional product offers, benefits of the upsell or cross-sell items.

- *Features:* Easy add-to-cart options, discounts for bundled purchases.

8. Post-Purchase Thank You Page

- *Purpose:* To thank the customer for their purchase and provide additional engagement opportunities.

- *Content:* Thank you message, next steps (e.g., how to use the product), and customer support contact information.

- *Features:* Links to user guides, social media pages, and referral programs.

9. Customer Feedback/Review Page

- *Purpose:* To gather feedback and reviews from customers.

- *Content:* Request for a review or feedback, easy-to-use forms or survey links.

- *Features:* Incentives for leaving reviews (e.g., discount on future purchases), and links to review platforms.

Summary of Webpages for a Product Launch Funnel:

1. **Pre-Launch Content Pages:** Build anticipation and capture early leads.

2. **Landing Page:** Convert visitors into leads with a compelling value proposition.

3. **Thank You Page (for Lead Capture):** Acknowledge leads and provide next steps.

4. **Sales Page:** Persuade visitors to purchase with detailed product information.

5. **Checkout Page:** Facilitate the secure and easy purchase process.

6. **Order Confirmation Page:** Confirm the order and provide purchase details.

7. **Upsell/Cross-Sell Page:** Offer additional products to increase order value.

8. **Post-Purchase Thank You Page:** Thank the customer and provide further engagement opportunities.

9. **Customer Feedback/Review Page:** Gather reviews and feedback from customers.

By incorporating these pages into your product launch funnel, you can create a seamless and effective journey that guides potential customers from initial interest to final purchase and beyond, maximizing your chances of a successful product launch.

MODULE 5: 5-Page Book Launch Funnel with Upsells

To structure a 5-page book launch funnel with three upsells, you can design the following flow:

Page 1: Main Sales Page

- *Purpose:* To introduce and sell the main product, your book.

- *Content:*

  - Compelling headline

  - Book cover image

  - Engaging description of the book's content and benefits

  - Author bio

  - Testimonials or endorsements

  - Clear call-to-action (CTA) to purchase the book

- *Features:*

  - Buy Now button with pricing information

  - Secure payment options

  - Limited-time bonus offer to create urgency

  - Opt-in form for additional exclusive content (e.g., a free chapter)

Page 2: Upsell 1 Page

- *Purpose:* To offer a complementary product related to the book, such as a workbook or guide.

- *Content:*

  - Description of the upsell product and its benefits

  - How it complements the main book

  - Testimonials or user reviews (if available)

  - Clear CTA to add this product to the order

- *Features:*

  - Add to Order button with pricing information

  - Special discount or bundle price

Page 3: Upsell 2 Page

- *Purpose:* To offer another related product, such as access to an exclusive webinar or online course.

- *Content:*

  - Detailed description of the webinar or course

  - Benefits and what participants will learn

  - Testimonials or endorsements

  - Clear CTA to purchase access

- *Features:*

  - Add to Order button with pricing information

  - Limited-time offer or discount for immediate purchase

Page 4: Upsell 3 Page

- *Purpose:* To offer a high-value product, such as a personalized coaching session or a signed copy of the book.

- *Content:*

  - Detailed description of the high-value offer

  - Unique benefits and exclusive nature of the offer

  - Clear CTA to add this product to the order

- *Features:*

  - Add to Order button with pricing information

  - Special discount or added bonus for purchasing the upsell

Page 5: Order Confirmation Page

- *Purpose:* To confirm the purchase and provide next steps.

- *Content:*

  - Thank you message for the purchase

  - Order summary with details of the purchased products

  - Information on what to expect next (e.g., shipping details, access information for digital products)

- *Features:*

  - Links to further engagement (e.g., join a readers' community, follow on social media)

- Offer to refer a friend for additional bonuses or discounts

Summary of the 5-Page Book Launch Funnel with Upsells:

1. **Main Sales Page:** Sells the main product (your book).

2. **Upsell 1 Page:** Offers a complementary product (e.g., a workbook).

3. **Upsell 2 Page:** Offers another related product (e.g., a webinar or online course).

4. **Upsell 3 Page:** Offers a high-value product (e.g., personalized coaching or a signed copy).

5. **Order Confirmation Page:** Confirms purchase and provides next steps.

This funnel structure is designed to maximize the value of each customer by presenting additional relevant offers that complement the main product, encouraging more purchases and higher overall order values.

MODULE 6: Funnel Components: Squeeze Page & Autoresponder

In this module, we will explore the critical components of an effective marketing funnel: the squeeze page and autoresponder. These elements are essential for capturing leads and nurturing them into loyal customers.

Squeeze Page

Purpose: A squeeze page is designed to capture the contact information of potential customers, primarily their email addresses. It's a pivotal component of your funnel as it initiates the relationship with your prospects.

Content:

1. **Compelling Headline:** Grab the visitor's attention with a headline that clearly communicates the value they will receive.
2. **Engaging Offer:** Present a valuable offer that entices the visitor to provide their contact information. This could be a free eBook, a special report, a checklist, or access to a webinar.
3. **Brief Description:** A short paragraph or bullet points explaining the benefits of the offer.
4. **Opt-In Form:** A form where visitors can enter their name and email address to receive the offer.

5. **Clear Call-to-Action (CTA):** A prominent button or link that directs the visitor to submit their information, such as "Get Your Free Report Now" or "Join the Webinar."

Features:

1. **Minimal Distractions:** Remove any unnecessary navigation or links that could divert the visitor's attention away from the opt-in offer.
2. **Visuals:** Use images or videos that support the offer and make the page more visually appealing.
3. **Trust Elements:** Include testimonials, trust badges, or privacy assurances to alleviate any concerns about sharing personal information.

Autoresponder

Purpose:

An autoresponder is an automated email sequence that nurtures leads by delivering valuable content and building a relationship with them over time. It helps maintain engagement with your audience and guides them through the buying process.

Components:

Welcome Email:

Purpose: To thank the subscriber for opting in and deliver the promised offer.

Content: A warm welcome message, a link to the free offer, and a brief introduction to what they can expect in future emails.

Educational Emails:

Purpose: To provide valuable information, tips, and insights related to your niche, building credibility and trust.

Content: Articles, how-to guides, videos, or case studies that address common pain points and offer solutions.

Engagement Emails:

Purpose: To encourage interaction and engagement with your content.

Content: Invites to webinars, surveys, polls, or requests for feedback.

Promotional Emails:

Purpose: To present special offers, discounts, or new product launches to your subscribers.

Content: Highlight the benefits of the offer, include testimonials or case studies, and provide a clear CTA to purchase or sign up.

Follow-Up Emails:

Purpose: To remind subscribers of the offer and encourage them to take action if they haven't already.

Content: Restate the benefits, address common objections, and include a sense of urgency (e.g., limited-time offer).

Features:

Personalization: Use the subscriber's name and tailor the content to their interests or behavior.

Timing and Frequency: Schedule emails to be sent at optimal times and intervals to keep the audience engaged without overwhelming them.

Tracking and Analytics: Monitor open rates, click-through rates, and conversions to measure the effectiveness of your email campaigns and make adjustments as needed.

Summary of Funnel Components: Squeeze Page and Autoresponder

Squeeze Page:

Purpose: Capture contact information of potential customers.

Content: Compelling headline, engaging offer, brief description, opt-in form, and clear CTA.

Features: Minimal distractions, supporting visuals, and trust elements.

Autoresponder:

Purpose: Nurture leads with valuable content and guide them through the buying process.

Components: Welcome email, educational emails, engagement emails, promotional emails, and follow-up emails.

Features: Personalization, optimal timing and frequency, and tracking and analytics.

By effectively using squeeze pages and autoresponders, you can build a robust marketing funnel that captures leads, nurtures relationships, and ultimately drives conversions and sales.

Module 7: Best Funnel Builders for Creating Highly Converting Funnels

In this module, we will explore some of the best funnel builders available in the market today. These tools are designed to help you create highly converting funnels that guide your potential customers through the buying journey seamlessly. The right funnel builder can significantly enhance your marketing efforts, streamline your processes, and boost your conversion rates.

Key Features to Look for in a Funnel Builder

When choosing a funnel builder, consider the following essential features:

1. Ease of Use: An intuitive, user-friendly interface that doesn't require advanced technical skills.
2. Customization: Flexibility to design funnels that match your brand's aesthetics and specific needs.
3. Templates: A variety of pre-designed templates for different types of funnels, such as lead generation, sales, webinar, and product launch funnels.
4. Integrations: Compatibility with your existing tools and platforms, including email marketing services, payment gateways, and CRM systems.
5. Analytics: In-depth reporting and analytics to track the performance of your funnels and make data-driven decisions.

6. Support: Access to reliable customer support and comprehensive resources like tutorials and documentation.

Top Funnel Builders

ClickFunnels

Overview: ClickFunnels is one of the most popular funnel builders, known for its ease of use and comprehensive features. It's ideal for marketers, entrepreneurs, and businesses looking to create high-converting sales funnels without needing technical expertise.

Key Features:

- Drag-and-drop editor
- Extensive template library
- Built-in email marketing and automation
- A/B testing
- Integration with major payment gateways
- Affiliate management through Backpack

Pros:

- User-friendly interface
- All-in-one solution for building and managing funnels
- Active community and extensive resources

Cons:

- Higher pricing compared to some competitors
- Limited customization options for advanced users

Leadpages

Overview: Leadpages is a versatile tool that allows you to create landing pages, pop-ups, and alert bars. It's particularly well-suited for lead generation funnels and offers robust features to optimize your conversion rates.

Key Features:

- Drag-and-drop builder
- Mobile-responsive templates
- Built-in conversion guidance (Leadmeter)
- Integration with popular email marketing and CRM tools
- A/B testing
- Real-time analytics

Pros:

- Affordable pricing plans
- Easy to use, even for beginners
- Strong focus on lead generation and conversion optimization

Cons:

- Limited functionality for building complex sales funnels
- Some users report limited design flexibility

Kartra

Overview: Kartra is an all-in-one marketing platform that includes funnel building as one of its core features. It's designed to handle various aspects of online business, including email marketing, membership sites, and helpdesk management.

Key Features:

- Drag-and-drop funnel builder
- Comprehensive marketing automation
- Membership site creation
- Video hosting and management
- Built-in affiliate management
- Detailed analytics and reporting

Pros:

- All-in-one platform with a wide range of features
- Strong focus on automation and integration
- Excellent customer support

Cons:

- Steeper learning curve due to extensive features
- Higher cost compared to standalone funnel builders

Builderall

Overview: Builderall is a comprehensive digital marketing platform that offers a variety of tools, including a funnel builder, website builder, email marketing, and more. It's designed for entrepreneurs and small businesses looking to manage all their online marketing needs in one place.

Key Features:

- Drag-and-drop page builder
- Sales funnels and checkout pages
- Email marketing automation
- Webinar hosting
- CRM system
- E-commerce integration

Pros:

- Affordable all-in-one solution
- Wide range of features and tools
- Regular updates and improvements

Cons:

- Interface can be overwhelming for beginners
- Some users report occasional bugs and performance issues

GetResponse

Overview: GetResponse is primarily known as an email marketing platform, but it also offers a robust funnel builder called Autofunnel. It's designed to help you create complete sales funnels with ease, from lead generation to sales and follow-ups.

Key Features:

- Pre-built funnel templates
- Drag-and-drop editor
- Email marketing and automation
- Webinar hosting
- E-commerce tools
- Detailed analytics

Pros:

- Easy to use with a focus on simplicity
- Integration with major e-commerce platforms
- Affordable pricing plans

Cons:

- Limited advanced customization options
- Primarily geared towards small to medium-sized businesses

Summary

Choosing the right funnel builder is crucial for creating highly converting funnels that drive your business growth. The tools listed above—ClickFunnels, Leadpages, Kartra, Builderall, and GetResponse—each offer unique features and benefits suited to different needs and budgets. By understanding the strengths and limitations of each, you can select the funnel builder that best aligns with your business goals and marketing strategies.